THE ART OF PAPER WEAVING

46 COLORFUL, DIMENSIONAL PROJECTS

ANNA SCHEPPER AND LENE SCHEPPER

Quarry Books
100 Cummings Center, Suite 406L
Beverly, MA 01915

quarrybooks.com • www.craftside.net

ACKNOWLEDGMENTS

We would like to thank the readers of our blog, PaperMatrix, for comments and inspiration. We owe special thanks to Carol Parssinen who challenged us to make our first woven sphere.

Thank you to Betsy Gammons, Joy Aquilino, Heather Godin, Kathy Brock, and the entire Quarry team for fruitful and dedicated cooperation.

Thank you to Annette Juhl and Ellen Dahl (Tivoli, Copenhagen), René Mønster (Cirkus Baldoni), and Mikkel Knudsen (Cirkusmuseet), for thoughtful reviews and expedient response.

Thank you to our families and friends for their love and interest in the project. Special thanks to Nikolaj, partner of Anna, and Poul Erik, husband of Lene and father of Anna, for help and support.

Quarto is the authority on a wide range of topics.

Quarto educates, entertains and enriches the lives of our readers—enthusiasts and lovers of hands-on living.

www.QuartoKnows.com

10 9 8 7 6 5 4 3 2

ISBN: 978-1-63159-039-9

Digital edition published in 2015
eISBN: 978-1-62788-316-0

Library of Congress Cataloging-in-Publication Data

Schepper, Anna.
  The art of paper weaving : 46 colorful, dimensional projects : includes practice
paper & full-size templates / Anna Schepper & Lene Schepper.
-- Digital edition.
    pages cm
  Includes bibliographical references and index.
  ISBN 978-1-63159-039-9
  1. Paper ribbon work. 2. Weaving. I. Schepper, Lene. II. Title.
  TT850.5.S334 2015
  746.1'4--dc23

2015000437

Design: Paul Burgess
All photography by Anna and Lene Schepper with the exception of page 70 (middle, right), Danish Cirkusmuseet. The Tivoli theme and the use of the images are in agreement with and approved by Tivoli, Copenhagen.

Access downloadable project templates at http://www.quarrybooks.com/pages/paper-weaving.

Printed in China

CONTENTS

PREFACE

Paper weaving is a thriving tradition in Denmark and Norway but is unknown in many other countries. In the United States, this magical craft, much loved by the Victorians, has passed into oblivion during the last 100 years. Anyone who has ever woven a paper heart understands its magic, when all of a sudden a beautiful geometrical object arises in front of you. Understanding this tradition and technique is a must for any paper lover. As essential as origami is for the Japanese, so too is paper weaving for the Danes.

We want to expose the tradition to a new generation of paper crafters and introduce its origin, but also reconstruct its geometries, further expand its possibilities, and harmonize with modern requests. The projects in this book represent our interpretations of several wondrous inspirations: exotic places, festive sceneries, and natural wonders. The objects can be used in daily life—as a mobile for a baby crib or container for your favorite keepsakes. They can be featured in festive scenarios as decorations or just to induce a smile on everyone's face.

Paper weaving is a craft that the whole family can participate in and enjoy. The different projects in *The Art of Paper Weaving* are created to allow easy accessibility for the beginner, but more challenges also await the skilled crafter. The expression "practice makes perfect" has never been truer when it comes to paper weaving. Our book contains a substantial collection of woven-paper projects, so we can introduce many techniques and tricks that are important to a novice paper weaver. It is essential to thoroughly read and understand the instructions before starting your paper project. We have strived to provide instructions as precisely as possible, and they might seem overwhelming at first, but be prepared: some models are time consuming and have a high level of difficulty.

We wish you all the best with your future paper projects and hope that you will find our favorite craft as fun and riveting as we do. Don't panic, keep a cool head, be patient, and enjoy yourself. It is just for fun.

—Anna and Lene

A BRIEF HISTORY OF PAPER WEAVING

You may have seen a red-and-white woven-paper heart basket, a tradition so embedded in the Danish culture that schoolchildren are taught to make them. The woven hearts come in many shapes and sizes, but they all have two base colors neatly woven together to form the basket. In the mid-nineteenth century, Hans Christian Andersen, the famous author of the fairy tales "The Little Mermaid," "The Ugly Duckling," and many others, brought the concept of a woven paper heart home to Denmark from his travels in Europe.

After such a magnificent introduction from their already internationally famous favorite son, the Danes came to love the woven heart, and it grew in popularity during the next fifty years. At the beginning of the twentieth century, the woven heart had reached the point of being an essential Danish tradition.

We have always been fascinated with this tradition. Devoted to create new patterns and matching colors and textures of all varieties, we set out to learn more about our favorite hobby.

We have traced the likely origin of woven-paper art to somewhere in the countries of Germany, Switzerland, and Austria. From there, the craft came to the United States with the immigrants in the early nineteenth century. In general, one could claim that the Germanic countries served as a melting pot of multiple ideas connecting and creating the woven-paper art form. Many varieties of this tradition are found today in folk-art museums and collections. Traditional woven paper objects fall into two categories: the woven heart basket and the "heart and hand" friendship and love token, the latter being a very popular art form in the Victorian age, particularly within the United States. Not just a pretty decoration, however, the paper objects had an intention: they were gifts or tokens of love for family, friends, and lovers. When one sees these woven-paper objects, it is not hard to imagine that the recipient would have been mesmerized by the intricacy, colors, and exquisiteness of these paper objects. Many were inscribed with verses, such as "Hand and heart / Will never part / When this you see / Remember me." A German verse found on paper gloves mixes hand/finger and love/faithfulness as well: "Auf Dise Finger Thun Ich Schrieben, Das Ich dir vill Treü ver Bleiben" (Peesch 1983, 116), meaning, "On these fingers writes he, that I will to thee forever faithful be."

A woven paper heart like one made by Hans Christian Andersen around 1860; the original is in the collection of the Hans Christian Andersen Museum in Odense, Denmark.

Opposing triangular notches in two pieces of paper was used for joining documents in the nineteenth century.

Going back in time, the initial technique used to join two pieces of paper is based on the principle of cutting opposing triangular notches, then joining them by slipping one point over the other to secure the merge. This was a "method commonly used to join documents in the pre-stapler, pre–paper clip, white-flour-paste world of the nineteenth century. It is easy to imagine that someone who happened to join two documents of different colors in this way for expediency's sake noticed the decorative possibilities and began experimenting" (May 2006, 62).

During the Biedermeier period in Germany (1815–1848), when Hans Christian Andersen was on his grand tour, many new influences were emerging onto society. When the German writer and statesman Johann Wolfgang von Goethe published *The Sorrows of Young Werther* in 1774, Romanticism—an intellectual and aesthetic movement that emphasized the imagination and emotions—was becoming popular, and thus the symbol of the heart was being implemented into popular culture. At about the same time, Friedrich Fröbel (1782–1852), a famous German pedagogue and founder of the kindergarten, believed that learning the language of geometry in youth would provide a common ground for all people (Brostermann 1997; Täubner 2012) and emphasized the technique of paper weaving.

In Denmark and the rest of Scandinavia, the legend of Hans Christian Andersen's introduction of paper weaving has kept the tradition alive and thriving today, connected with simplicity and imagination, unlike other European countries and the United States, where the tradition slowly fell into oblivion. Leslie S. May (2006, 63) writes that the demise of the art of woven paper following the U.S. Civil War "could almost certainly be attributed to the flood of colorful, commercially produced chromolithographed cards and scraps that appeared on the market around 1870."

During the twentieth century, paper weaving continued to be developed and explored in Denmark. Many paper artists have presented their version of the woven heart and pushed the possibilities of the craft, and among them, we have been particularly inspired by two talented artists: first is the architect Hans Henrik Koch (1873–1922), godson of Hans Christian Andersen and a man so knowledgeable about geometrical shapes that he took the idea of woven paper beyond the strict and limiting geometries of the heart shape and applied the technique to a multitude of two-dimensional shapes. In the mid-1960s, a young man named Jesper Gundermann (1949–2006)—our second inspiration—created three-dimensional woven paper objects in the shape of a cone. Understanding his calculation methods has paved the way for the many of the three-dimensional objects presented in this book.

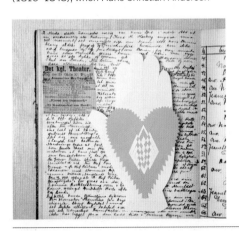

Heart-in-hand paper token resembling the tokens common in the United States during the period 1840–1860; the original (shown in Leslie S. May's article in *Folk Art* magazine) is in the collection of New York City's American Folk Art Museum.

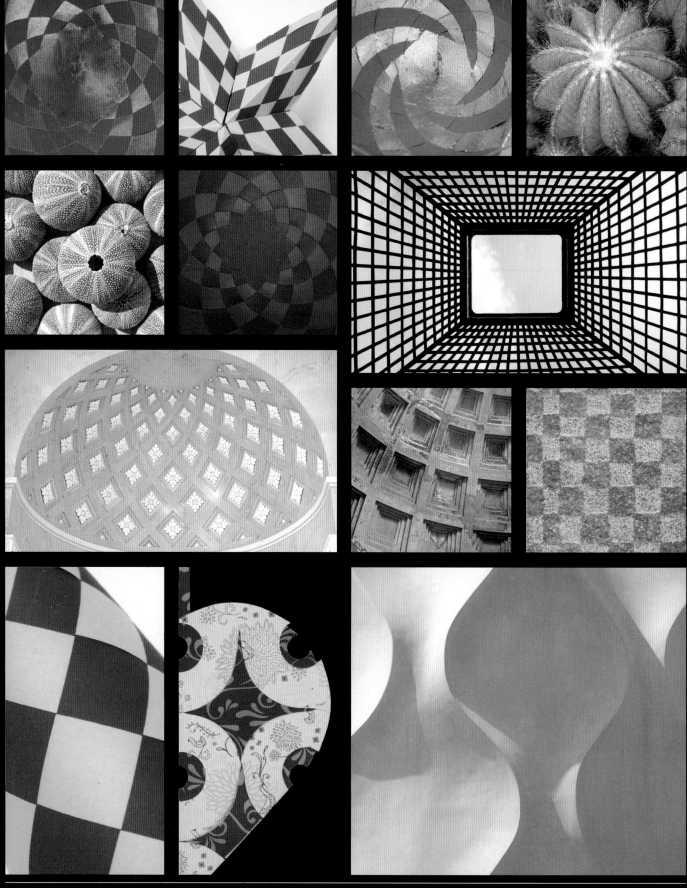